FLUTE

BEST of BEETHOVEN

FLUTE

CONTENTS

Instrumental arrangements by David Pearl

Cherry Lane Music Company
Director of Publications: Mark Phillips
Publications Coordinator: Rebecca Skidmore

ISBN: 978-1-60378-252-4

Visit our website at www.cherrylaneprint.com

FÜR ELISE

FLUTE

By Ludwig van Beethoven

Moderately

rit.

PIANO CONCERTO NO. 3
First Movement

FLUTE

by Ludwig van Beethoven

PIANO SONATA NO. 14 "MOONLIGHT"

First Movement

FLUTE

By Ludwig van Beethoven

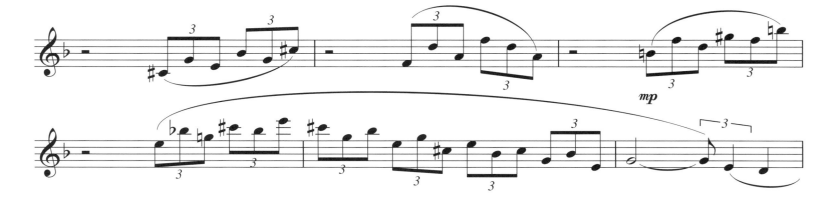

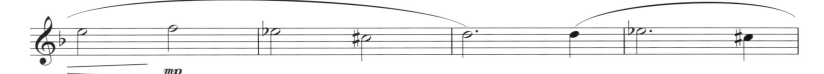

PIANO TRIO NO. 7 "ARCHDUKE"
Third Movement

FLUTE

By Ludwig van Beethoven

Slowly

SYMPHONY NO. 2
Second Movement

FLUTE

By Ludwig van Beethoven

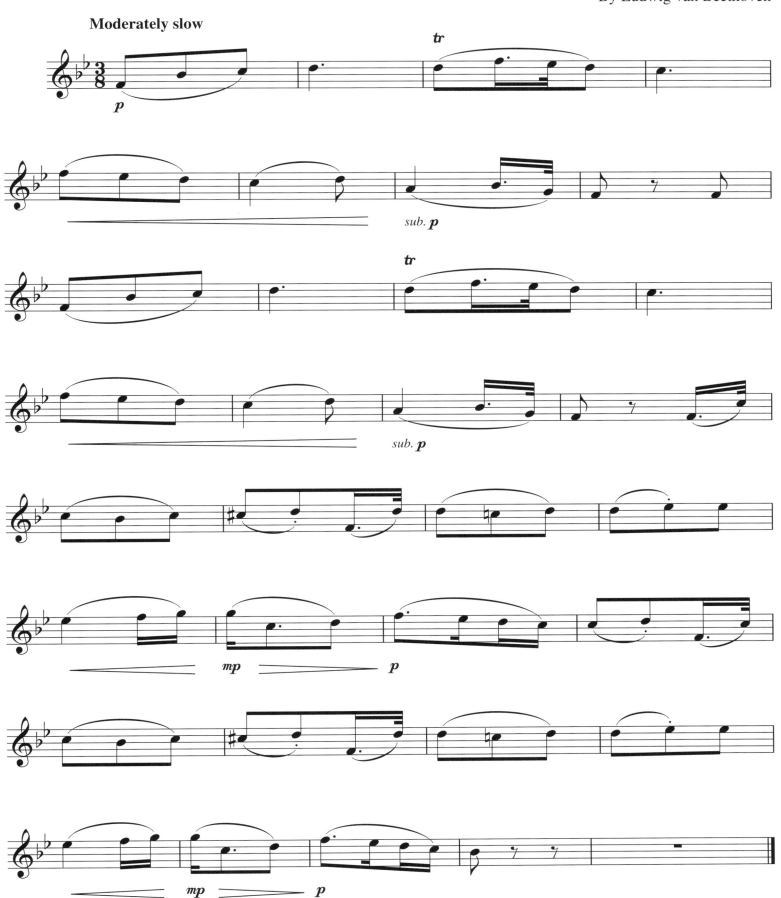

SYMPHONY NO. 3
Second Movement

FLUTE

By Ludwig van Beethoven

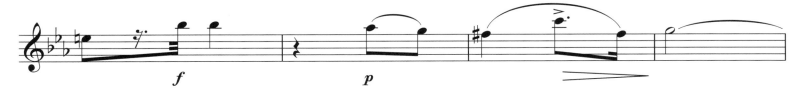

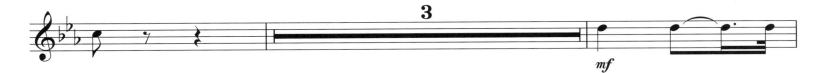

SYMPHONY NO. 5

First Movement

FLUTE

By Ludwig van Beethoven

SYMPHONY NO. 6

Fifth Movement

FLUTE

By Ludwig van Beethoven

Slower

SYMPHONY NO. 7
Second Movement

FLUTE

By Ludwig van Beethoven

TRACK 10

SYMPHONY NO. 8
Second Movement

FLUTE

By Ludwig van Beethoven

Moderately

Orchestra   *Play*

18

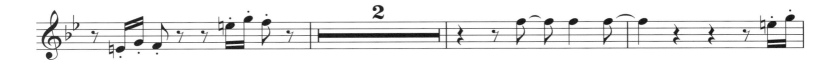

cresc.

TURKISH MARCH
from *The Ruins of Athens*

FLUTE

By Ludwig van Beethoven

Moderately fast

cresc. poco a poco

SYMPHONY NO. 9

Fourth Movement "Ode to Joy"

FLUTE

By Ludwig van Beethoven

great songs series

This legendary series has delighted players and performers for generations.

Great Songs of the Fifties

Features rock, pop, country, Broadway and movie tunes, including: All Shook Up • At the Hop • Blue Suede Shoes • Dream Lover • Fly Me to the Moon • Kansas City • Love Me Tender • Misty • Peggy Sue • Rock Around the Clock • Sea of Love • Sixteen Tons • Take the "A" Train • Wonderful! Wonderful! • and more. Includes an introduction by award-winning journalist Bruce Pollock.
02500323 P/V/G......................................$16.95

Great Songs of the Sixties, Vol. 1 – Revised

The updated version of this classic book includes 80 faves from the 1960s: Angel of the Morning • Bridge over Troubled Water • Cabaret • Different Drum • Do You Believe in Magic • Eve of Destruction • Monday, Monday • Spinning Wheel • Walk on By • and more.
02509902 P/V/G......................................$19.95

Great Songs of the Sixties, Vol. 2 – Revised

61 more '60s hits: California Dreamin' • Crying • For Once in My Life • Honey • Little Green Apples • MacArthur Park • Me and Bobby McGee • Nowhere Man • Piece of My Heart • Sugar, Sugar • You Made Me So Very Happy • and more.
02509904 P/V/G......................................$19.95

Great Songs of the Seventies, Vol. 1 – Revised

This super collection of 70 big hits from the '70s includes: After the Love Has Gone • Afternoon Delight • Annie's Song • Band on the Run • Cold as Ice • FM • Imagine • It's Too Late • Layla • Let It Be • Maggie May • Piano Man • Shelter from the Storm • Superstar • Sweet Baby James • Time in a Bottle • The Way We Were • and more.
02509917 P/V/G......................................$19.95

Great Songs of the Eighties – Revised

This edition features 50 songs in rock, pop & country styles, plus hits from Broadway and the movies! Songs: Almost Paradise • Angel of the Morning • Do You Really Want to Hurt Me • Endless Love • Flashdance...What a Feeling • Guilty • Hungry Eyes • (Just Like) Starting Over • Let Love Rule • Missing You • Patience • Through the Years • Time After Time • Total Eclipse of the Heart • and more.
02502125 P/V/G......................................$18.95

Great Songs of the Nineties

Includes: Achy Breaky Heart • Beautiful in My Eyes • Believe • Black Hole Sun • Black Velvet • Blaze of Glory • Building a Mystery • Crash into Me • Fields of Gold • From a Distance • Glycerine • Here and Now • Hold My Hand • I'll Make Love to You • Ironic • Linger • My Heart Will Go On • Waterfalls • Wonderwall • and more.
02500040 P/V/G......................................$16.95

Great Songs of Broadway

This fabulous collection of 60 standards includes: Getting to Know You • Hello, Dolly! • The Impossible Dream • Let Me Entertain You • My Favorite Things • My Husband Makes Movies • Oh, What a Beautiful Mornin' • On My Own • People • Tomorrow • Try to Remember • Unusual Way • What I Did for Love • and dozens more, plus an introductory article.
02500615 P/V/G......................................$19.95

Great Songs for Children

90 wonderful, singable favorites kids love: Baa Baa Black Sheep • Bingo • The Candy Man • Do-Re-Mi • Eensy Weensy Spider • The Hokey Pokey • Linus and Lucy • Sing • This Old Man • Yellow Submarine • and more, with a touching foreword by Grammy-winning singer/songwriter Tom Chapin.
02501348 P/V/G......................................$19.99

Great Songs of Classic Rock

Nearly 50 of the greatest songs of the rock era, including: Against the Wind • Cold As Ice • Don't Stop Believin' • Feels like the First Time • I Can See for Miles • Maybe I'm Amazed • Minute by Minute • Money • Nights in White Satin • Only the Lonely • Open Arms • Rikki Don't Lose That Number • Rosanna • We Are the Champions • and more.
02500801 P/V/G......................................$19.95

Great Songs of Country Music

This volume features 58 country gems, including: Abilene • Afternoon Delight • Amazed • Annie's Song • Blue • Crazy • Elvira • Fly Away • For the Good Times • Friends in Low Places • The Gambler • Hey, Good Lookin' • I Hope You Dance • Thank God I'm a Country Boy • This Kiss • Your Cheatin' Heart • and more.
02500503 P/V/G......................................$19.95

Great Songs of Folk Music

Nearly 50 of the most popular folk songs of our time, including: Blowin' in the Wind • The House of the Rising Sun • Puff the Magic Dragon • This Land Is Your Land • Time in a Bottle • The Times They Are A-Changin' • The Unicorn • Where Have All the Flowers Gone? • and more.
02500997 P/V/G......................................$19.95

Great Songs from The Great American Songbook

52 American classics, including: Ain't That a Kick in the Head • As Time Goes By • Come Fly with Me •Georgia on My Mind • I Get a Kick Out of You • I've Got You Under My Skin • The Lady Is a Tramp • Love and Marriage • Mack the Knife • Misty • Over the Rainbow • People • Take the "A" Train • Thanks for the Memory • and more.
02500760 P/V/G......................................$16.95

Great Songs of the Movies

Nearly 60 of the best songs popularized in the movies, including: Accidentally in Love • Alfie • Almost Paradise • The Rainbow Connection • Somewhere in My Memory • Take My Breath Away (Love Theme) • Three Coins in the Fountain • (I've Had) the Time of My Life • Up Where We Belong • The Way We Were • and more.
02500967 P/V/G......................................$19.95

Great Songs of the Pop Era

Over 50 hits from the pop era, including: Every Breath You Take • I'm Every Woman • Just the Two of Us • Leaving on a Jet Plane • My Cherie Amour • Raindrops Keep Fallin' on My Head • Time After Time • (I've Had) the Time of My Life • What a Wonderful World • and more.
02500043 Easy Piano..$16.95

Great Songs of 2000-2009

Over 50 of the decade's biggest hits, including: Accidentally in Love • Breathe (2 AM) • Daughters • Hanging by a Moment • The Middle • The Remedy (I Won't Worry) • Smooth • A Thousand Miles • and more.
02500922 P/V/G......................................$24.99

Great Songs for Weddings

A beautiful collection of 59 pop standards perfect for wedding ceremonies and receptions, including: Always and Forever • Amazed • Beautiful in My Eyes • Can You Feel the Love Tonight • Endless Love • Love of a Lifetime • Open Arms • Unforgettable • When I Fall in Love • The Wind Beneath My Wings • and more.
02501006 P/V/G......................................$19.95

Prices, contents, and availability subject to change without notice.

7777 W. BLUEMOUND RD. P.O. BOX 13819 MILWAUKEE, WI 53213

www.cherrylane.com

0610

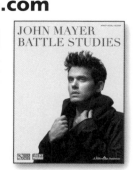